New CLAIT
Unit 3
Electronic Communication
The Course Book

CGP's Course Books offer a step-by-step approach
to help you really get to grips with New CLAIT.

Each topic is explained using everyday language,
with plenty of worked examples, handy hints and practical tasks.

Exactly what you need —
perfect for even the most 'computer-phobic' learners.

CONTENTS

Published by Coordination Group Publications Ltd.

Endorsed by OCR for use with OCR Level 1 Certificate for IT users - New CLAIT specification.

ISBN 1 84146 328 0

Groovy website: www.cgpbooks.co.uk

With thanks to Kate Manson and Robert Edwards for the proof-reading.

Jolly bits of clipart from CorelDRAW.

Printed by Elanders Hindson, Newcastle upon Tyne.

With thanks to Microsoft for permission to use screenshots from MS Internet Explorer, and MS Windows XP.

Text, design, layout and original illustrations © Coordination Group Publications 2004.

All rights reserved.

Contributors:
Jo Anson
Charley Darbishire
Dominic Hall
Simon Little
Rachel Selway
Jennifer Underwood

What is New CLAIT?

Here's a page to let you know what this book is all about.

New CLAIT is a Computer Course for Beginners

In New CLAIT, you'll learn how to make computers work for you, so you can use things like:

- <u>word processors</u> — to write letters
- <u>spreadsheets</u> — to do your household accounts
- <u>databases</u> — to organise information
- <u>e-mail</u> — to keep in touch with people all over the world

Just Have a Go, You Won't Break it

The <u>key</u> to learning about computers is to <u>try things</u>.
Don't be afraid of it — you <u>won't break</u> the computer with a mouse and keyboard.
You'd need to open it up and pour a cup of tea inside to break it.

This book will take you through everything
<u>step-by-step</u>. You'll be doing things all the time.

When you've got to <u>do things</u>,
you'll find <u>numbered shapes</u> like this.

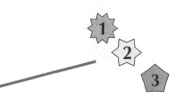

There are also <u>practice exercises</u> in each section,
so you can see how you'd do in a real New CLAIT test.

Read this bit if you are a Tutor

1) We've used <u>Office XP</u> and <u>Windows XP Professional</u> for this
   book, but most things will be the same for older versions.

2) To keep things <u>simple</u> we've concentrated on one way of doing things instead
   of confusing people with five different ways to do the same thing.

3) There is a <u>CD</u> which accompanies this
   series of books. It contains files the student
   will need for the worked examples, practice
   exercises and exams.

   Note: For this unit, we haven't
   provided answer files as the exercises
   are all practical tasks like sending
   e-mails and navigating web pages.

Just relax and enjoy the ride...

This book tells you everything you need to pass New CLAIT Unit 3.
The first section is a reminder of the basic computer skills you'll need for the New CLAIT course.

The Bits of a Computer

Here's what each bit of your computer does, just in case you've forgotten.

The Parts of a Computer Do Different Jobs

Here's a computer — and all the bits are labelled.

Monitor — looks like a **TV** screen. What you're working on is displayed on it.

System box — the 'brain' of the computer, where all the bits and pieces that make it work can be found. You put CDs and disks in here, and plug all the other computer parts into the back.

Printer — used to make a paper copy of what's on your screen, like letters or photos.

CDs and floppy disks — can be used to store your work. You can put them into a different computer and your work will appear.

Mouse — when you move this over your desk, a little arrow on the screen will move too. You can use it to select and change different things on the screen.

Keyboard — has keys with letters and numbers on that you press to enter information, e.g. to write a letter.

Boring... show me the complicated stuff now...

OK so you probably knew all this stuff already. You'll get to the new bits in a minute. If you needed a little reminder, don't worry... it'll soon come back to you.

The Bits of a Computer

This page covers some of the common computing terms you're likely to hear a lot.

Computers come in Different Shapes

Laptops are handy little computers that you can fold up, carry about in a bag and use on the train, should you fancy. They're as good as normal computers, just smaller.

Notebooks are like laptops, but smaller and a bit less powerful. (Still plenty good enough for us normal folks though.)

Computers are made of Hardware and Software

HARDWARE is all the physical bits of a computer — not just the obvious bits like the monitor, keyboard and printer, but also the gubbins inside that make it work.

SOFTWARE is all the programs in a computer that make it do different things — i.e. the instructions that tell the computer what to do. You can buy new software on CDs.

For example, 'Microsoft Word' is a program which lets you write letters and things. A computer game is another program, where the keys you press might guide a character round a special world. Nice.

Here are Some Terms You'll Need to Know

1) Programs, like 'Microsoft Word' or 'Microsoft Excel', are called applications.

2) Files are made with applications. They contain the things you make — a file from a word processor like 'Microsoft Word' will be lots of text, and a file from a drawing program will be a picture.

3) A folder is a place where you can store files or applications. They're really useful for organising your computer.

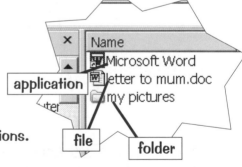

'Microsoft Windows' is a special program called an 'operating system' — it lets you interact with the computer, open and close other programs, and generally control what's going on — useful.

Programs like 'Microsoft Windows' let you do loads of things without having to understand what's really going on.

You'll be seeing a lot more of these things...

It's good to know what all the terms on this page mean, but the main thing is knowing how to use the actual applications. As long as you can make them work for you, you're doing fine.

Using the Keyboard

You'll probably recognise the keyboard by now. It's not hard to spot.

All Keyboards Look the Same (More or Less)

The big bit with the letters on is always the same — it's the same arrangement as on a typewriter. So if you've used a typewriter before, you should pick it up really easily.

Don't worry about these keys. They're called function keys and do special things in different programs.

These are navigation keys, and do things like taking you to the start or end of your work. Don't worry about most of these — you won't use many apart from 'Delete'.

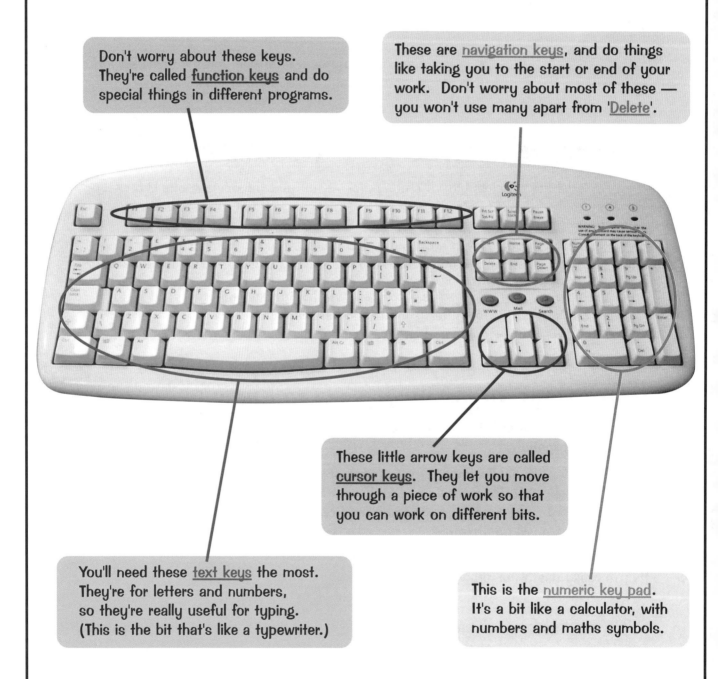

These little arrow keys are called cursor keys. They let you move through a piece of work so that you can work on different bits.

You'll need these text keys the most. They're for letters and numbers, so they're really useful for typing. (This is the bit that's like a typewriter.)

This is the numeric key pad. It's a bit like a calculator, with numbers and maths symbols.

Whatever you do, don't press the BIG RED button...

Don't worry about accidentally pressing one of the keys that we've said you won't need. There's no "self-destruct", "ejector seat" or big "DON'T PRESS" button on a standard keyboard.

Using the Keyboard

Remind yourself about the special keys on the keyboard as well.

Some Keys are Really Special

Here are some of the keys you'll find really useful when you're typing:

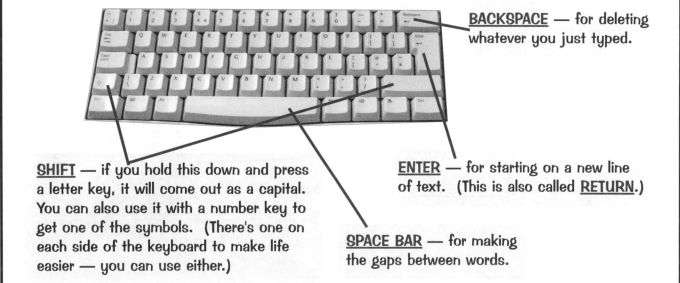

BACKSPACE — for deleting whatever you just typed.

SHIFT — if you hold this down and press a letter key, it will come out as a capital. You can also use it with a number key to get one of the symbols. (There's one on each side of the keyboard to make life easier — you can use either.)

ENTER — for starting on a new line of text. (This is also called **RETURN**.)

SPACE BAR — for making the gaps between words.

Have a Go at Using the Keyboard

Learning to type is really slow to begin with, but you'll soon get better with practice. If you need a bit more practice, have a look at New CLAIT Unit 1 — Using a Computer.

Open a word-processing application and have a go at typing:

- Make sure you're typing accurately. It doesn't matter if you're slow.
- You don't have to whack the keys — find out how lightly you can press a key and still make it work.
- Make sure you know how to use the four special keys above.

Get lots of typing practice...

You'll be getting plenty of typing practice in this book with all the e-mails you'll be sending. By the end of the book, you'll be a super-fast typist. You might even forget how to use a pen...

Get Used to the Mouse

If you've met the mouse before, you'll know it's not a small furry animal by now.

First, Catch Your Mouse...

This is a mouse.

This is its right button.

This is its left button.

This is a mouse mat.

The mouse has a nice <u>rounded top</u> that you put your palm on,
and a couple of <u>buttons</u> at the top where your fingers go. Like this.

...Then Push it Around a bit

1) To use your mouse, all you have to do is <u>push</u> it around on your desk.
    (You'll find that it <u>glides</u> along nicely on top of a foamy <u>mouse mat</u>.)

2) Underneath the mouse will be a little <u>ball</u> or a little <u>red light</u>.
    This bit tells the computer how you are <u>moving</u> the mouse.

3) As you move the mouse, a little <u>arrow</u> on your screen
    moves about. This arrow is called a <u>pointer</u>.

Pointers look a bit like this.
(But they're about ten times <u>tinier</u>.)

When you're using <u>writing software</u>, like 'Microsoft
Word', your pointer will look like this, but a lot smaller.

Don't worry if your pointer looks <u>different</u> to the ones above. It'll be really obvious —
the pointer is the thing that <u>moves about</u> on your screen when you move the mouse.

Don't be alarmed, but there's a mouse on your desk...

In fact, once you've got used to moving it around, the mouse is a really useful thing for just
about everything you do in New CLAIT. Make friends with yours right now.

Get Used to the Mouse

For this book you'll need to use both the left and right mouse buttons. Read on...

You'll use the Left Mouse Button most of the time

You normally just 'click' the mouse button — give it a quick press
and then take your finger off again — you'll hear a little clicking noise.

- The left mouse button can 'select' things. This means that when you move the pointer over something and click your left mouse button, you'll make it 'alive' and useable.

- If you 'double-click' the left mouse button — quickly click on something twice — you'll be able to open programs and make things work.

You'll need the Right Mouse Button too

You'll need to click the right mouse button to do some of the things in this book, like saving and printing pictures from the Internet. There's more on this on pages 33, 41 and 43.

Try this Quick Activity for Learning Mouse Control

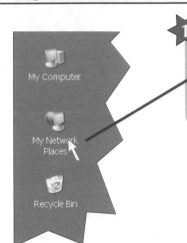

1 Move the mouse around until the pointer on the screen is on top of an icon. (An icon is a little picture, representing a file or application.)

 Click the left mouse button once. The icon will get darker — become highlighted. This means you have selected it.

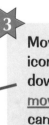 Move the pointer over a different icon. Press the left mouse button down and keep it held down. Then move your mouse and you'll find you can drag the icon about. Useful.

 If you 'double-click' on an icon (move your pointer to it and do a quick 'click click'), you'll make it open.

These fingers were made for clicking...

If you've done New CLAIT Units 1 and 2 this should be pretty easy by now —
all you've got to remember is: left once selects, left twice opens, left-hold-move drags.

Internet Basics

You've probably heard of the Internet, even if you're not sure how to use it yet.
It's a great way to find information, and send e-mail messages.

The Internet is a lot of Computers Linked Together

1) The Internet is a huge network of computers joined together by telephone lines and satellites.

2) If you want to send e-mail messages or look at websites, you need to connect to the Internet.

3) If you're accessing the Internet from home, you'll need to connect your computer to the Internet first. You normally do this by clicking on an icon to connect to your ISP (Internet Service Provider) — a company like AOL or Wanadoo.

4) Your college computers will probably be permanently connected to the Internet, so all you need to do is open your browser...

You use a Browser to Look at Stuff on the Internet

The Internet contains pages of information and pictures — these are called websites.
They are stored on different computers all over the world.

A browser is a program which lets you move about between different websites.
One of the most common browsers is 'Internet Explorer'.
You'll learn more about it in Section 4, but here's how to open it:

 Click on 'Start', move your mouse up to 'Programs', then across to 'Internet Explorer'.

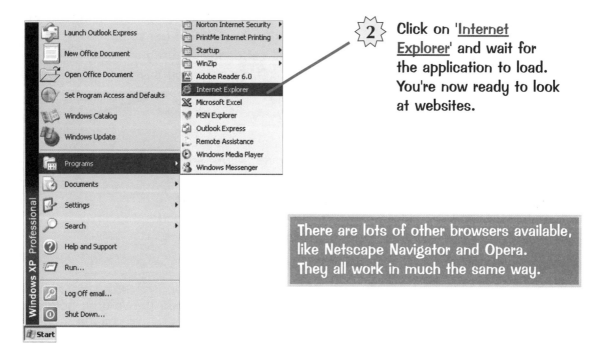

2 Click on 'Internet Explorer' and wait for the application to load. You're now ready to look at websites.

There are lots of other browsers available, like Netscape Navigator and Opera. They all work in much the same way.

I've always wanted to be an Internet Explorer...

The network of websites is really called the World Wide Web (WWW), but most people just call it the Internet. You could call it Mavis if you wanted, but no one would understand.

E-mail Basics

E-mailing seems to have taken over from letter-writing these days.
It's a really quick way to send messages, and keep in touch with people all over the world.

E-mail _is_ Electronic Mail

E-mail is just like writing a letter, but you send it using the
Internet, and it only takes a few minutes to arrive. You can
even send people pictures and other files from your computer.

E-mail — faster than carrier pigeon.

There are Different Ways _to_ E-mail

1) Some people use e-mail on a website (like Hotmail).
    Your messages are stored on an Internet site. You can log on
    to this site from any computer to read your e-mails and send messages.

2) At college you'll probably use an e-mail application like 'Outlook Express' which
    stores messages on your computer. This makes it easier to manage your e-mails,
    but you'll only be able to get at them when you're connected to the college system.

Open _your_ E-mail Software Using the 'Start' Menu

Before you can e-mail people, you'll need to open your e-mail software.

1 Click on 'Start', move up to 'Programs',
then across to 'Outlook Express'.

2 Click on 'Outlook
Express'. Ta da —
you've opened it.

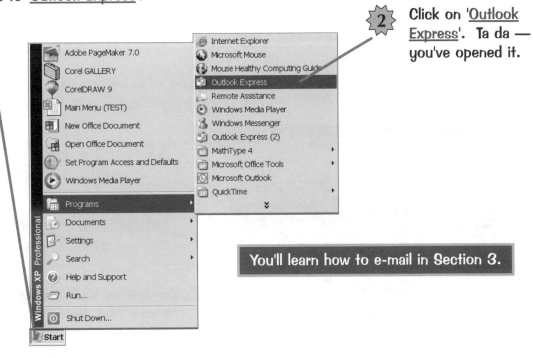

You'll learn how to e-mail in Section 3.

E-mailing beats snail-mailing...

Once you get the hang of e-mailing, it's a really cheap and easy way to keep in
touch with people, even if they live somewhere like Fiji, or the South Pole.

Outlook Express

It's time to get to grips with using e-mail software. We've used Outlook Express on these pages, but all e-mail applications have similar features, so don't worry if you use a different one.

Outlook Express has a Front Page

When you first open Outlook Express (see page 9), you'll get a page that looks a bit like this:

Here are your folders (see below). You click on a folder to open it.

You'll see a list of names — these are the people in your address book.

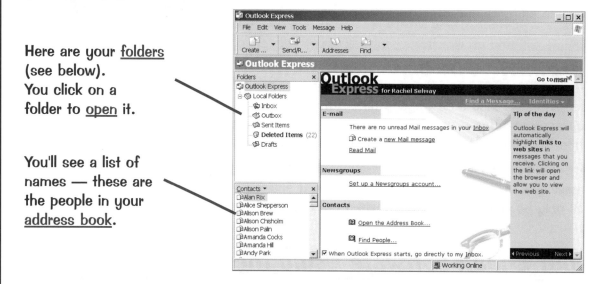

You have Different Folders for Different E-mails

E-mails are stored in folders, just like the folders you store other computer files in.

(1) Click on 'Local Folders' to see how many e-mails you have in each of the following folders:

Inbox — where received e-mails live until you delete them.

Outbox — where e-mails you've written live before you connect to the Internet to send them.

Sent Items — e-mails that you've written and sent.

Deleted Items — e-mails that you've deleted from your inbox.

Drafts — e-mails that you started to write and decided to finish later.

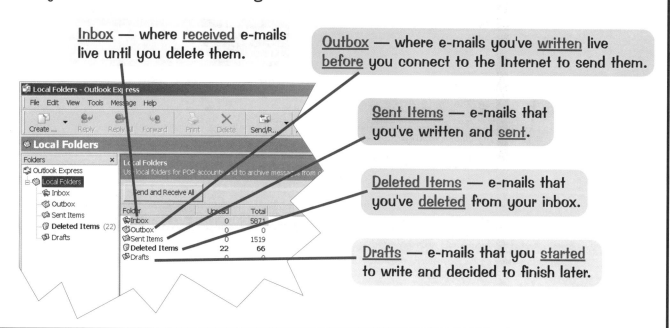

E-by-gum mail...

All those folders are pretty useful. Once you start getting hundreds of e-mails, you'll find it really handy to organise your stuff properly. Otherwise there'll be e-mails all over the place...

Writing New E-mails

It's really easy to e-mail someone, as you'll see now...

There are Six Stages to Sending an E-mail

Here's how to write and send an e-mail:

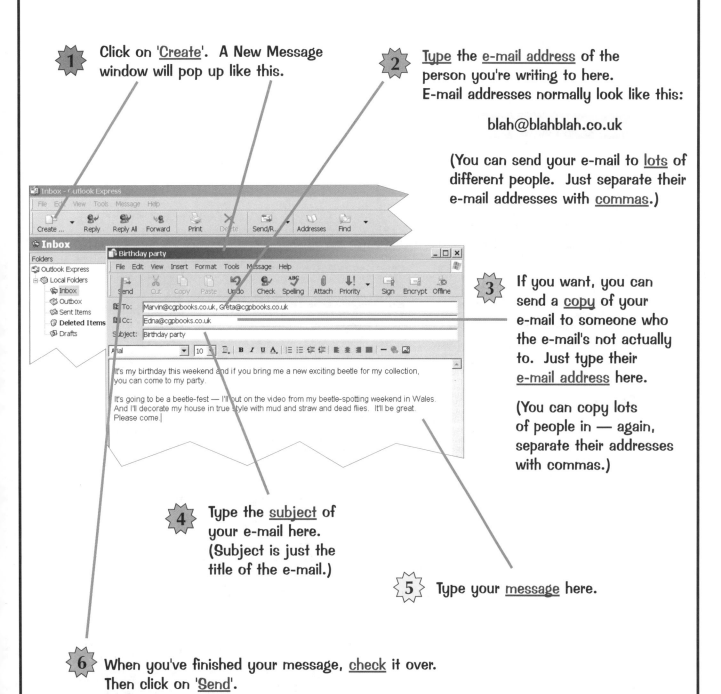

1 Click on 'Create'. A New Message window will pop up like this.

2 Type the e-mail address of the person you're writing to here. E-mail addresses normally look like this:

blah@blahblah.co.uk

(You can send your e-mail to lots of different people. Just separate their e-mail addresses with commas.)

3 If you want, you can send a copy of your e-mail to someone who the e-mail's not actually to. Just type their e-mail address here.

(You can copy lots of people in — again, separate their addresses with commas.)

4 Type the subject of your e-mail here. (Subject is just the title of the e-mail.)

5 Type your message here.

6 When you've finished your message, check it over. Then click on 'Send'.

Go on, send an e-mail to someone right now...

Here's a word of advice — take care when typing e-mail addresses. One spelling mistake and your e-mail won't get where it's meant to go. It might go to a different person. So be careful.

Reading E-mails

It won't be long before you're getting e-mails. Here's how to read them.

New E-mails Appear in Your Inbox

When you receive new e-mails, they'll turn up in your inbox, and stay there until you delete them.

1 Click on 'Inbox' to open it.

This is what your inbox looks like when it's got loads of e-mails in it:

This shows who the e-mail's from.

This is what it's about (the "subject").

This is when it was sent.

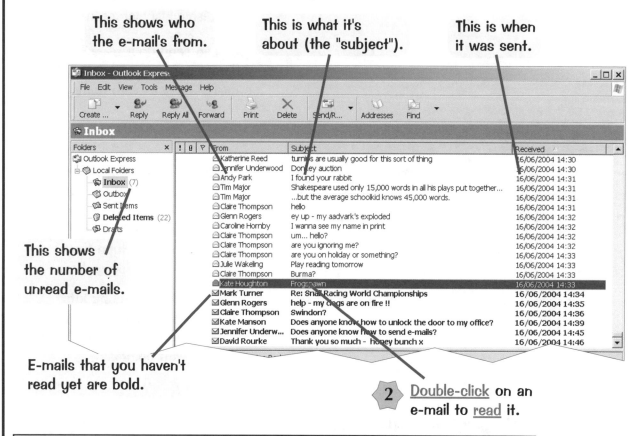

This shows the number of unread e-mails.

E-mails that you haven't read yet are bold.

2 Double-click on an e-mail to read it.

E-mails Don't Always Turn up Automatically

E-mails turn up automatically when you're connected to a network of computers at work or college. But usually they won't turn up until you connect to the Internet:

Just click on 'Send/Receive'.

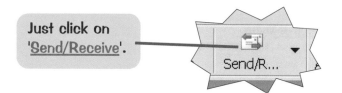

When you click on this button, you'll connect to the Internet — automatically sending any e-mails you've written and receiving any that have been sent to you.

E-mail's great for everyone... except postmen...

Unless they learn to deliver letters in 0.03 seconds, the days of the Royal Mail are numbered. Having said that, you can't send parcels by e-mail, so there's still one use for good old snail mail.

Replying to E-mails

Now you know how to read e-mails, here's how to reply...

Replying to E-mails is Easier than Sending Them

1 From your inbox, select the e-mail that you want to reply to by clicking on it.

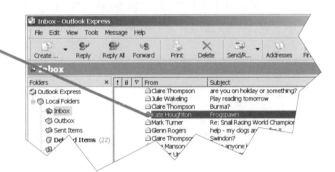

2 Click on 'Reply'.

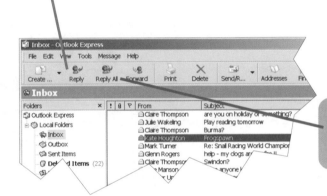

If the message has been sent to lots of people, you can reply to all of them at once, by clicking 'Reply All'.

3 You'll get a new window like this that contains the original message. Just write your reply above it. The address and subject will already be filled in.

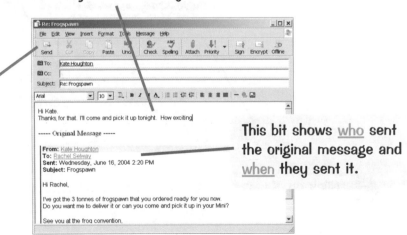

4 When you've finished writing your message, click on 'Send'.

This bit shows who sent the original message and when they sent it.

Oh what an easy page...

If you tend to write e-mails you don't want others to read, try not to accidentally click on 'Reply to All'. You don't want everyone to find out about your office romance the wrong way...

Forwarding E-mails

Got a really good e-mail? Want to share it with the world? Well now you can...

Forwarding E-mails is Just Like Replying

If you read an e-mail and think that someone else might like to read it too, you can send it to them. This is called forwarding. You can even add your own message to the forwarded e-mail.

1 In your inbox, click on the message you want to forward.

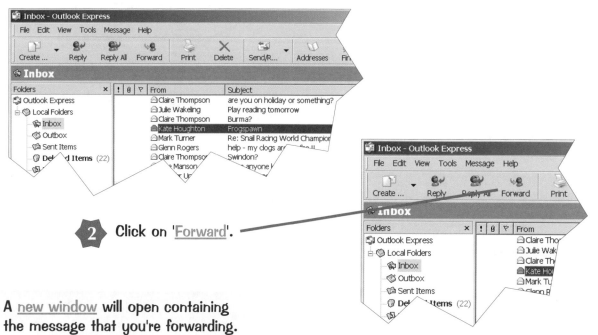

2 Click on 'Forward'.

A new window will open containing the message that you're forwarding.

3 Fill in the address of the person you want to send the message to.

4 If you want to, add your own notes above the original message.

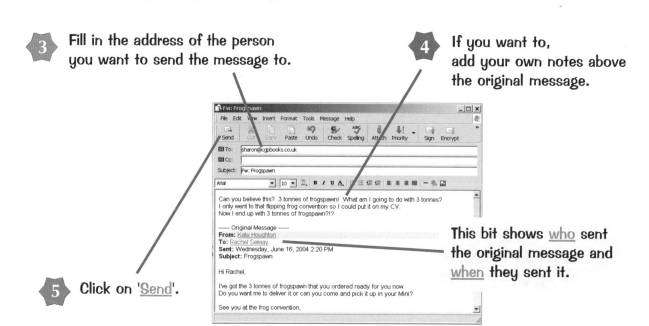

This bit shows who sent the original message and when they sent it.

5 Click on 'Send'.

Your inbox shows your forwarded messages...

Your inbox will tell you which e-mails you've forwarded and replied to. A blue forwards arrow means it's been forwarded and a purple backwards arrow means it's been replied to. How nice.

Address Books

You can make sending e-mails even simpler by using an address book.

Address Books Store E-mail Addresses

E-mail programs have <u>address books</u> for you to store your e-mail addresses in — just like a normal address book. Here's how to <u>fill</u> it with e-mail addresses in Outlook Express.

1 Click on '<u>Addresses</u>'.

2 You'll get a new <u>window</u> like this. Click on '<u>New</u>', then click on '<u>New Contact</u>'.

3 You'll get a window like this. Carefully <u>fill in</u> the name and e-mail address of your contact. (The '<u>Display</u>' bit fills itself in.)

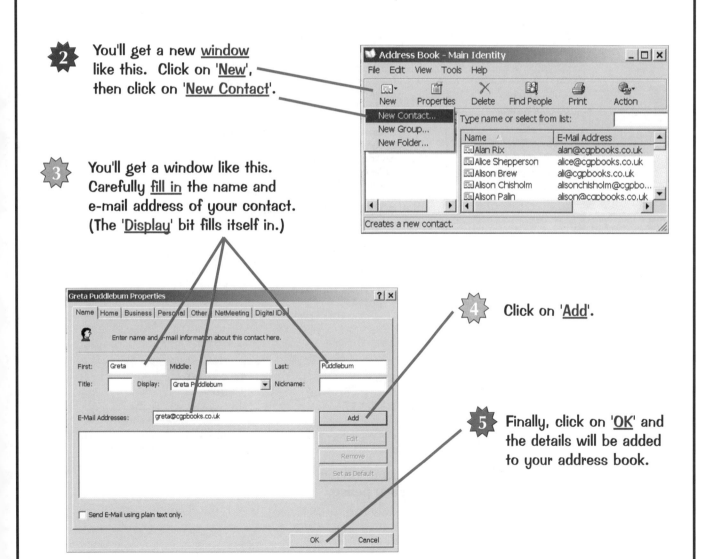

4 Click on '<u>Add</u>'.

5 Finally, click on '<u>OK</u>' and the details will be added to your address book.

Better than writing on the back of your hand...

Computer address books are so handy. Imagine what life would be like without them...
You'd have to read your own handwriting for a start, or trust your own memory. Hmmm...

Address Books

Often you'll receive an e-mail from someone that you'd like to add to your address book.

You can Easily Add Someone who has E-mailed You

When you receive e-mails from people who aren't
in your address book, this is how to add them...

 Click on Inbox.
Your received e-mails
should appear to the right.

 Now, click your right mouse
button on their message.
Yes, I said "right" mouse button.

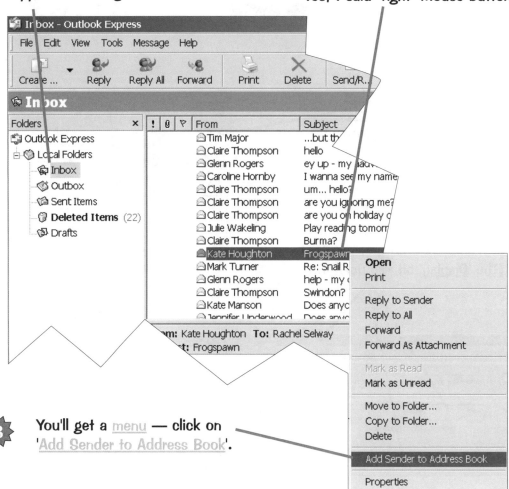

 You'll get a menu — click on
'Add Sender to Address Book'.

Their details are then automatically added
to your address book. Easy peasy.

You won't leave this address book on the bus...

If someone in your address book changes their e-mail address, or even their name,
don't panic. Just click on 'Addresses', select their name, then click on 'Properties'.
You'll be able to edit their details and soon everything will hunky-dory once again.

Address Books

It's really simple to send an e-mail to someone in your address book.

Send E-mails Using Your Address Book

 1 Click on 'Create' (see page 11).

2 You'll get a New Message window to write in.
Click on 'To'.

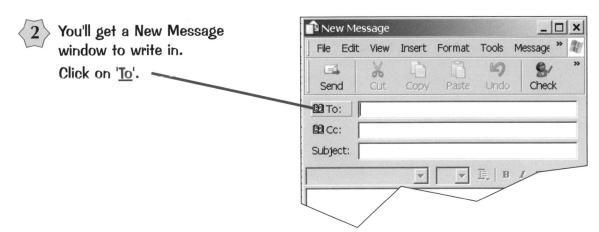

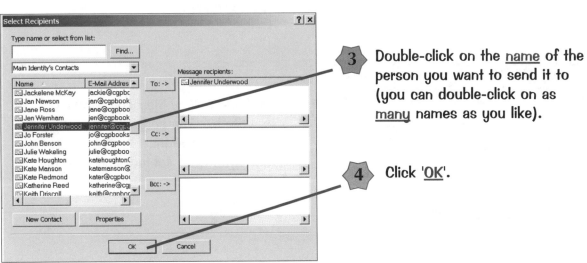

3 Double-click on the name of the person you want to send it to (you can double-click on as many names as you like).

4 Click 'OK'.

5 The address part is filled in for you. Just write your subject and message.

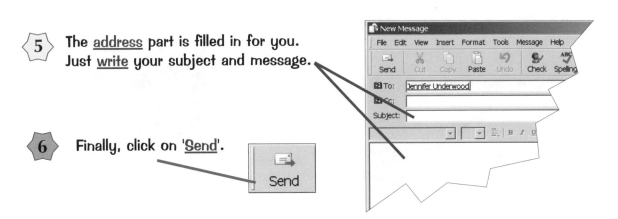

6 Finally, click on 'Send'.

Now all you need is some addresses to write to...

This is where you see how useful address books are. They save you the hassle of typing out people's e-mail addresses (and making mistakes). Instead, you just click on the name. Easy.

Address Books

Wow... here's another page about address books. Address books must be pretty useful then.

There's a Quick Way to use your Address Book

You may have a list of contacts in the bottom left of your e-mail screen.
These are the people in your address book.

 1 Double-click on the name of the
person you want to write to.

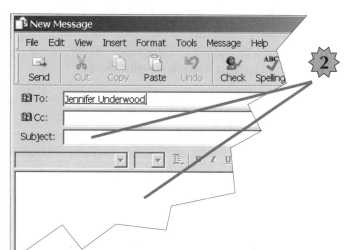

2 You'll get a New Message window
to write in. The address part will
already be filled in.
Just write your subject and message.

3 Click on 'Send'. So easy.

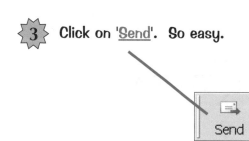

Frank was overrun with
e-mails from his admirers.

An address book can save you loads of time...

You don't have to learn both ways of using your address book. Choose the way that you find easiest to remember. And remember to use it, rather than typing in the address each time.

Section Three — Practice Exercises

It's time to try some practice exercises to see how much you've taken in so far.

For these exercises, you will need three or more e-mail addresses (including your tutor's) to send messages to. Ask your tutor for the addresses to use. You could use the addresses of other students in your class.

Exercise 1

1. Open your mailbox and create a new e-mail message to your tutor with the subject "**Success**".

2. Type in the following message:

   I have successfully accessed my e-mail account and this is the first of many e-mails that you will receive.

3. Add your name and centre number to the end of your message.

4. Check your message for errors and send this message to your tutor.

Exercise 2

1. Create a new e-mail message to send to your tutor and to be copied to two other addresses, with the subject "**Coffee and cakes**".

2. Type in the following message:

   There is a large cake sale happening at break time. Fancy a coffee and lots of cake?

3. Check your message for any errors and spelling mistakes and then send it to your tutor and the two other addresses.

   Note for tutor: Some of the recipients need to reply to this message for the exercise to continue.

4. Wait several minutes, then open your mailbox and check to see if you have any new messages. You should have some replies to your **Coffee and cakes** e-mail.

5. Reply to your messages by suggesting a place to meet.

Exercise 3

This exercise will work best if both recipients reply.

1. Create an e-mail message entitled "**Holiday**" to send to your tutor that will be copied to one other e-mail address.

2. Enter the following message:

   I am going to London next week for a mini-break. I am going to explore some of the museums and go to the West End. Can you recommend any good shows to see?

3. Check your message for any errors and send it.

4. Reply to any messages you receive about your holiday e-mail.

Section Three — Practice Exercises

It's not time for tea (or coffee) just yet... Not until you've done a tiny bit more practice...

Exercise 4

1.   Open your mailbox and create a new message to send to your tutor
       with the subject "**Web Courses**".

2.   Type in the following e-mail message:

> I am very interested in creating a website about my pet iguana.
> Can you recommend any web courses please? Are any starting soon?

The tutor needs to reply to this e-mail for the exercise to continue.

3.   Add your name and centre number to the end of the message.

4.   Check your message for errors and send it to your tutor.

5.   Check at regular intervals for a reply to the message.

6.   When you have received a reply, forward it to a new address (another tutor or student),
       adding the following text:

> I have just received this information. Is this useful to you?

Check your message for errors before sending it.

Exercise 5

1.   Open your mailbox and create a new e-mail message to send to your tutor
       with the subject "**Christmas Concert**".

2.   Type in the following message:

> There is a Christmas concert and carol service taking place on 18th December at 11am.
> Mince pies, Christmas cake and cups of tea will be available afterwards, plus lots of
> last-minute bargains including cards, plants and crafts.

3.   Add your name and centre number to the end of the message.

4.   Check your message for errors and send it to your tutor.

5.   Find an e-mail previously sent to you and forward it to a new address
       (another tutor or student), adding the following text:

> I thought you might be interested in the following information.

Check your message for errors before forwarding it to the new address.

Deleting E-mails

OK, so now you know how to do the basics when it comes to e-mail. Here's how to do more.

Deleting E-mails Stops You Running Out of Space

Over time, your inbox will fill up with messages.
You can delete the messages you don't need any more, to make more space.

Deleting messages is as simple as pressing a button:

 1 Select the message you want to delete by clicking on it.

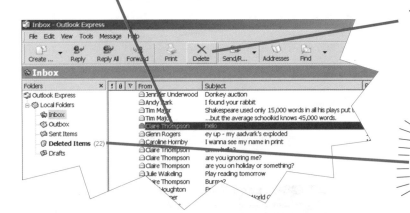

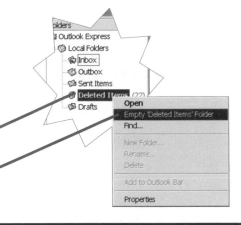 **2** Click on 'Delete'.
The message you delete will move from your inbox to the folder called 'Deleted Items'.

Don't get confused by this number. It shows the number of <u>unread</u> deleted messages, not the number of <u>deleted</u> messages.

 3 Don't worry if you delete something by mistake.
Click on 'Deleted Items'.

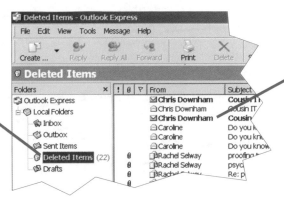

You'll see all the e-mails you've deleted.
Double-click on them to read them.

You can also move the message back into your inbox —
right click on the message, click on 'Move to Folder...' then on 'Inbox', then on 'OK'.

To permanently delete things you need to empty the 'Deleted Items' folder.

 4 To do this, click your right mouse button on 'Deleted Items'. Then click on 'Empty 'Deleted Items' Folder'. And it's done.

Deleting's fun — but remember to read them first...

If you're deleting e-mails to free up space on your computer, remember that it's e-mails with files attached that take up all the room — especially photos and music. Delete them first.

Printing E-mails

It's always useful to learn how to print things. Well, here's how to print e-mails.

You Can Print out your E-mails

It's often useful to have paper copies of important e-mails so that you can file them away.
That's when printing comes in handy. Just follow these instructions:

1 Select the message you want to print.

2 Click on 'Print'.

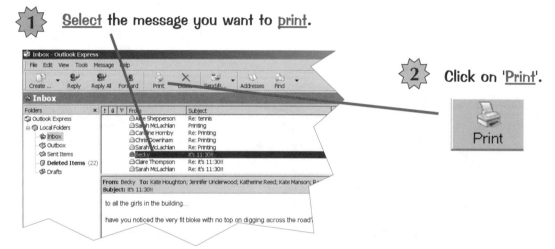

3 You'll see this screen.
Choose which printer to use, if you have a choice.
Choose how many copies you want to print.

4 Click on 'Print'.

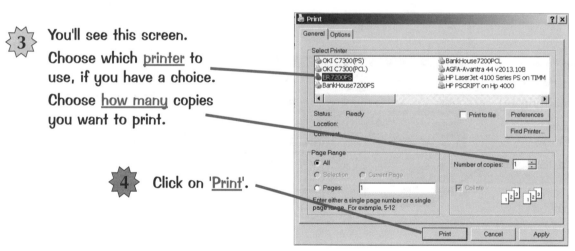

Your print-out will look something like this:

Your name
Who the e-mail's from
Who it's to
When it was sent
The e-mail's title ("subject")
The message itself

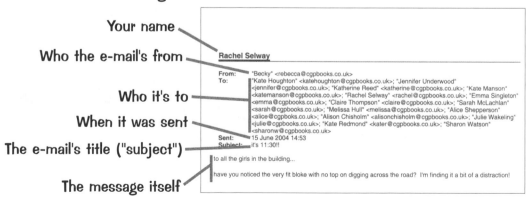

Printing... erm... can't think of anything more to add...

So as you can see, when you print an e-mail, it doesn't just print the message,
but also all the details like who it's from, when it was sent and so on. Useful.

Sending Attachments

Once you learn how to send <u>attachments</u>, you'll wonder how you ever lived without them.
You can e-mail photos, pictures, Word documents, Excel documents, music... It's amazing.

Attachments *are E-mailed Files*

Sending attachments is so <u>easy</u> — send one to someone in your class like this:

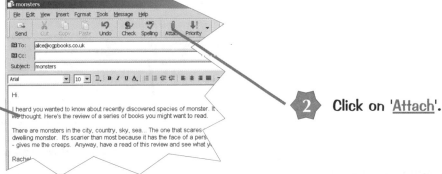

 <u>Write</u> a new e-mail
as you learnt on
page 11, but <u>don't</u>
click on 'Send'.

2 Click on '<u>Attach</u>'.

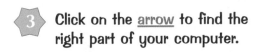 You'll get a <u>window</u> like this — you need to
<u>find</u> the file '<u>monster book review</u>' (it's on
the CD — ask your tutor where to find it).

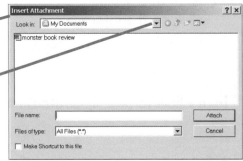

3 Click on the <u>arrow</u> to find the
right part of your computer.

4 <u>Click</u> on the place where it's stored, then
<u>double-click</u> on each <u>folder</u> until you get to the file.

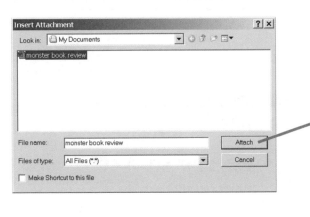

5 When you find the file
'<u>monster book review</u>', click on it,
then click on '<u>Attach</u>'.

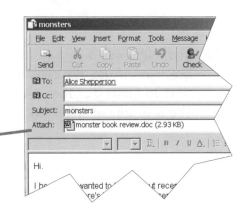

6 The attached file will now
appear below the subject.
Click on '<u>Send</u>'.

Staples and sellotape won't help you here...

You can attach more than one thing at once, if you like. Just repeat steps 2 to 5 before you
click on 'Send'. There's a limit to the amount of files you can attach though — not hundreds...

Receiving Attachments

It's always exciting to receive an attachment from somebody — it feels like your birthday.

Attachments are Obvious — Look for a Paperclip

If you ever look in your inbox and discover an e-mail has a little
paperclip next to it, then you've received an attachment. Wow.

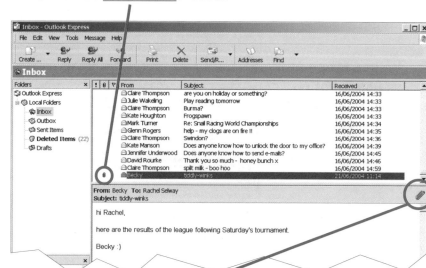

1 Get your tutor to
send you an e-mail
with the file 'Tiddly-
winks league table
results' attached.

2 From your inbox,
click on the message
to select it.

Here's how to open your attachment:

3 Click on this paperclip.
A menu will appear underneath.

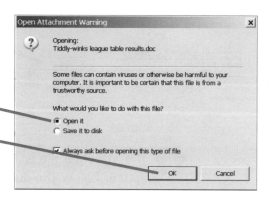

4 You'll see a file name.
Click on the file name.

5 You might see a warning message
like this. If you do, click on the circle
next to 'Open it'. Then click on 'OK'.
The attachment will open.

But beware — not all attachments are friendly...

Computer viruses are spread through attachments. If there's a virus in an attachment, and you
open it, then your computer will be infected. Don't panic though — they're pretty rare and easy
to avoid. Just don't open an attachment from someone you don't know, and delete the e-mail.

Saving Attachments

When you receive an attachment, you'll often want to save it somewhere for future reference.

You Can Save Your Attachments

Saving attachments is more or less like saving anything...

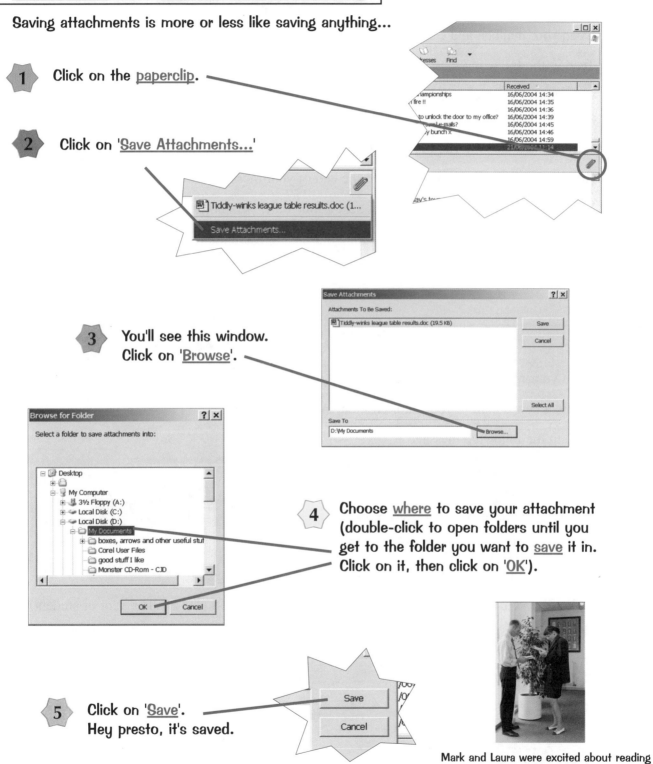

1 Click on the <u>paperclip</u>.

2 Click on '<u>Save Attachments...</u>'

> Tiddly-winks league table results.doc (1...
> Save Attachments...

3 You'll see this window. Click on '<u>Browse</u>'.

Save Attachments
Attachments To Be Saved:
Tiddly-winks league table results.doc (19.5 KB)
Save
Cancel
Select All
Save To
D:\My Documents   Browse...

Browse for Folder
Select a folder to save attachments into:
- Desktop
  - My Computer
    - 3½ Floppy (A:)
    - Local Disk (C:)
    - Local Disk (D:)
      - My Documents
        - boxes, arrows and other useful stuf
        - Corel User Files
        - good stuff I like
        - Monster CD-Rom - CJD
OK   Cancel

4 Choose <u>where</u> to save your attachment (double-click to open folders until you get to the folder you want to <u>save</u> it in. Click on it, then click on '<u>OK</u>').

5 Click on '<u>Save</u>'. Hey presto, it's saved.

Save
Cancel

Mark and Laura were excited about reading the "P45" attachment they'd been sent.

Save me... save me...

It's a good idea to save attachments somewhere. If you just leave them in your inbox, they'll be lost forever in a pile of old e-mails, and then accidentally deleted with that pile of old e-mails.

Section Three — Practice Exercises

It's time to practise e-mailing attachments. Give it a try and see how you get on.

Exercise 1

1. Open your mailbox and create a new message to your tutor with the subject "**Holiday Snaps**".

2. Type in the following message:

   Hi, we have just come back from our trip to London.
   I have attached a picture of Big Ben - it was fantastic to see it in real life.

3. Locate and attach the file **bigben.gif**.   Your tutor will tell you where to find this file.

4. Add your name and centre number to the end of your message.

5. Make sure a copy of your message is sent to one other person (another tutor or student).

6. Check your message for errors and send your message and attachment.

Exercise 2

1. Open your mailbox.

2. Create a new e-mail to your tutor entitled "**A Fun Day Out**".

3. Type in the following message:

   Hi, a group of us have just come back from a great day out at a theme park. We went on loads of rides and nearly all of us went on a really scary one. I have attached a picture someone took of us on the ride.

4. Locate and attach the file **scaryride.gif**

5. Add your name and centre number to the end of your message.

6. Make sure your message is copied to one other e-mail address (for another tutor or student).

7. Check your message for errors and send your message and attachment.

Section Three — Practice Exercises

There's another page of e-mail exercises here, so get stuck in and enjoy...

Exercise 3

1. Open your mailbox and create a new message to your tutor with the subject **"Camping"**.

2. Type in the following message:

    A group of us are going camping in the Lake District over the weekend of the 12th and 13th of July. We aim to do a couple of walks including Scafell Pike. We also have use of canoes on the Sunday, so we can have some fun on the water too. Do you want to come along?

3. Add your name and centre number to the end of the message.

4. Locate and attach the file **lakes.gif**.

5. Check your message for errors and send it to your tutor.

6. Find the message you sent entitled **"Camping"** and forward it to two other addresses, adding the following text:

    Would you be interested in a camping weekend in the Lakes?
    We have plenty of tents, you'd just need a sleeping bag.

    Check your message for errors before forwarding it to the new addresses.

Exercise 4

This final exercise involves deleting messages, so check with your tutor before starting it.

You need to tidy up your mailbox to reduce storage demands.

1. Make sure all attachments have been saved separately from the mailbox, in a separate folder on a floppy disk or folder on the hard disk.

2. Locate the messages that you have sent and print a copy of each message.

3. Now delete all sent messages (you have now got a printed copy for reference and any attachments are saved elsewhere).

4. Create a new message to send to your tutor entitled **"Storage Space"**.

5. Type in the following message:

    I have successfully printed and deleted all sent messages (saving all attachments first). You may wish to check this operation has been done.

6. Add your name and centre number to the end of the message.

7. Check your message for errors and send it to your tutor.

Browse a Web Page

You can use the Internet to find information about absolutely anything.
It's like a massive library full of books and magazines.

It's Easy to Start Browsing the Internet

 1 Open 'Internet Explorer' (see page 8 for a reminder).

> A web page will appear automatically, which is your 'homepage',
> — you'll see it every time you connect to the Internet.

This is an example of a web page.

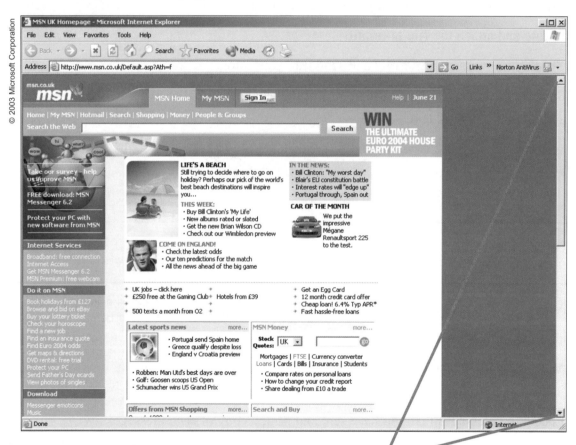

© 2003 Microsoft Corporation

 2 Click on these arrows to move up and down the
web page. (These "scroll bars" only appear if the
web page is taller or wider than the window.)

 3 When you've finished looking at the page,
click on this button to close Internet Explorer.

There are some things you can't do on the Internet...

But you can buy a car, find a recipe for snail stew, argue with strangers, do your banking, visit
a virtual zoo, auction your best friend, book a holiday, read a newspaper, start a romance...

Browse a Web Page

You're probably fed up of the homepage by now, so here's how you look at a different website.

To go Straight to a Website, you can type its Address

Every website has a unique address. They usually look like this: www.extremehoovers.co.uk

The www bit tells you you're using the World Wide Web.
The extremehoovers bit is the name of the website.
The co.uk means it's probably a company based in the UK.

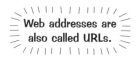
Web addresses are also called URLs.

You need to type web addresses exactly right, including the full stops, or they won't work.

1 Open 'Internet Explorer'.

2 Click your mouse inside the white address box.

3 Use the 'Backspace' key to delete the address that's already there.

4 Type in the address of the website you want to go to, exactly like this.

5 Now press 'Enter'.

6 Wait a few seconds ...

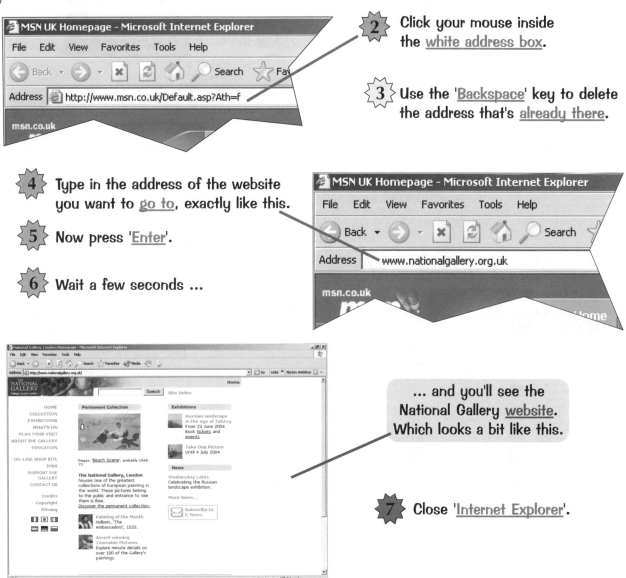

... and you'll see the National Gallery website. Which looks a bit like this.

7 Close 'Internet Explorer'.

© National Gallery Company Limited

Don't worry too much about addresses...

Don't panic if you can't remember what each bit of the Internet address means.
Just make sure you know how to type them into your browser so you can look at the sites.

Navigating the Web

Once you've reached a website, you can click on 'hyperlinks' to go to other pages that have the information that you want.

Hyperlinks take you to Other Web Pages

You're going to take a look at the National Gallery's pictures.

 Open 'Internet Explorer'.

 Type www.nationalgallery.org.uk into the address bar (see page 29 for help).

 Move the mouse over the word 'Collection' — the pointer arrow should change to look like a pointing finger — that means there's a hyperlink there.

 Click with the left mouse button.

© National Gallery Company Limited

Now a different page should open about the gallery's collection.

© National Gallery Company Limited

 Move your mouse over the new page to find another hyperlink that'll let you see some of the pictures in the collection.

 When the pointer arrow changes to a pointing finger, click with the left mouse button.

When you've finished browsing, close 'Internet Explorer'.

Now you're really surfing...

This is what people mean when they say they're 'surfing the Net' — you can use hyperlinks to move from one page to another, following the things that interest you most.

Navigating the Web

Your browser has some handy buttons that help you make the most of the Internet.

Browsers have Special Buttons to help you Navigate

 Open the webpage at www.nationalgallery.org.uk, as on the previous page.

 Click on the 'Collection' hyperlink. You should get this web page.

 Click on the 'Back' button to go back to the previous web page.

© National Gallery Company Limited

© National Gallery Company Limited

 Now click on the 'Home' button. This will take you back to your 'homepage' (see page 28).

'Refresh' and 'Stop' are Useful Too

You probably won't use these two as much as 'Back' and 'Home', but they do come in handy.

The 'Refresh' icon shows you the most updated version of a page. That's handy if you're looking at a news website, where the stories change every few minutes.

The buttons on your computer might look a bit different from these ones.

 'Stop' stops a page in the middle of loading — e.g. if it's taking too long, or you decide you don't want to look at it after all.

Don't get stuck in the Web...

There's a lot of fascinating stuff out there, but don't forget to stop surfing the Net from time to time so you can eat and sleep.

Storing Internet Addresses

"Bookmarking" websites that you visit a lot can save you loads of time.
It also helps you remember a good site you come across by accident.

You can Store your Favourite Internet Addresses

1 In Internet Explorer, type this address into the address bar: www.nmgw.ac.uk/wsm
Wait for the web page to load.

2 Click on 'Favorites'
on the menu bar.

Then click on
'Add to Favorites'.

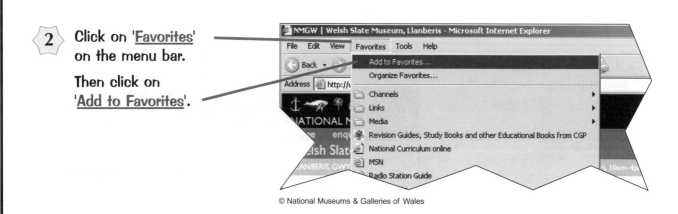

© National Museums & Galleries of Wales

3 This box lets you organise your Favourites in different folders.
Choose a folder to save the address in, and double-click to open it.

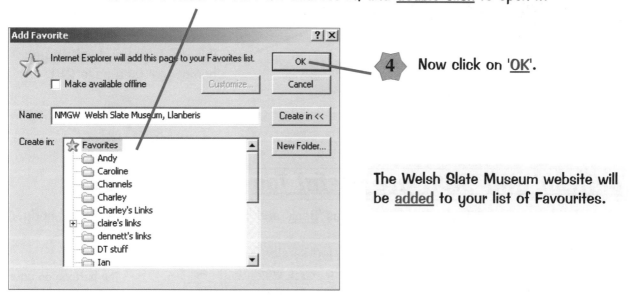

4 Now click on 'OK'.

The Welsh Slate Museum website will
be added to your list of Favourites.

5 Close 'Internet Explorer'.

Storing web addresses like this is called Bookmarking...

In the test, you might be asked to "bookmark" a web page. Don't be thrown by this
— it just means adding the page to your favourites list, i.e. exactly what we've done here.

Storing Internet Addresses

You can go back to your Favourite Sites

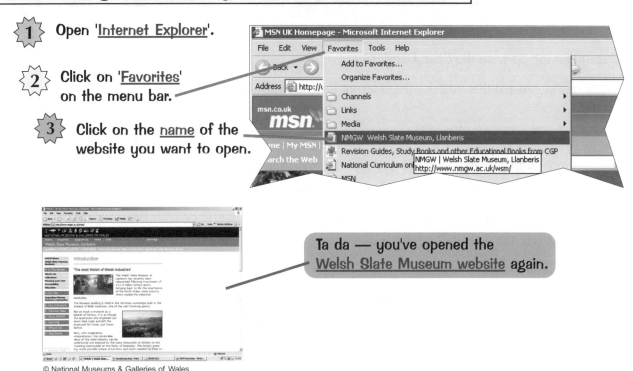

1 Open 'Internet Explorer'.

2 Click on 'Favorites' on the menu bar.

3 Click on the name of the website you want to open.

© National Museums & Galleries of Wales

Ta da — you've opened the Welsh Slate Museum website again.

You can also Remove Favourites

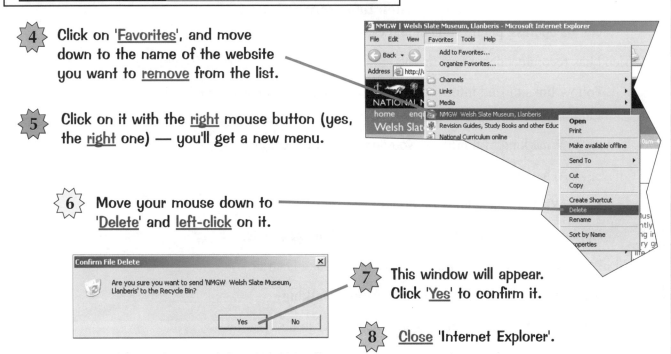

4 Click on 'Favorites', and move down to the name of the website you want to remove from the list.

5 Click on it with the right mouse button (yes, the right one) — you'll get a new menu.

6 Move your mouse down to 'Delete' and left-click on it.

7 This window will appear. Click 'Yes' to confirm it.

8 Close 'Internet Explorer'.

Confirm File Delete

Are you sure you want to send 'NMGW Welsh Slate Museum, Llanberis' to the Recycle Bin?

[Yes]   [No]

That right mouse button can be dead useful...

Right-clicking brings up some handy little menus, especially when you're using the Internet. Have a play with it — click around on a couple of pages, see what it comes up with.

Section Four — Practice Exercises

Now it's time to surf the Internet for some practice — lucky you.

Exercise 1

You are planning a trip to the Lake District.

A friend has suggested that you use the Internet to find information to help you plan your trip.

1.   Access the Lake District National Park website at www.lake-district.gov.uk

2.   Follow a link or links to find a page giving **weather forecast** information.
      Find out what the forecast is like for the next three or four days.

3.   When you have the information you need, use the **Back** button of your browser
      to return to the website's homepage.

You are thinking of staying in the village of Coniston.

4.   Follow links to find a page that lists **events** happening over the
      coming days. Find information about one or two events
      happening in the **Coniston** area.

5.   When you have the information you need, return to the site's homepage.

6.   Follow links to find information about **accommodation**.

7.   Find the contact details of **Coniston Information Centre**,
      e.g. its address, phone number and e-mail address.

A friend has recommended a visit to The Lake District Visitor Centre at Brockhole.

8.   Follow links to find information about the **Visitor Centre** at **Brockhole**.
      Find the answers to these questions:

      •   What kind of things can you do or see at the centre?

      •   What are the opening times?

      •   What are the admission prices?

9.   Bookmark the page about the Visitor Centre at Brockhole.

You'd like to do some walking while you are in the Lake District.

10.   Navigate the site to find information about **walking**.

11.   Try to find information about particular walks to do.

Section Four — Practice Exercises

Here are some more exciting exercises to keep you happy.

Exercise 2

You need to plan a trip to the Science Museum in London for a group of older children.

Go to the website at www.sciencemuseum.org.uk

Follow links on the website to find the information you need to answer these questions:

Q1. What are the **opening times** of the museum?

Q2. What are the **admission prices** of the museum?

Q3. What is the **address** of the museum?

Q4. What is the closest **tube station** to the museum?

Q5. Are there any cafes or restaurants there or will you need to take a packed lunch?

Q6. What special **exhibitions** are on? Find details of some of these exhibitions.

Exercise 3

You are planning a trip to Oxford. You are going to look for information on the university's website.

1. Go to the University of Oxford website, at www.ox.ac.uk

2. Follow a link to take you to a page for **visitors**.

3. Find information on **how to get to Oxford**.

4. Navigate the site to find a **map** of Oxford that shows all the **Colleges and Halls** in Oxford.

5. When you have finished, use the **Back** button of your browser to return to the University's homepage.

You'd like to find information about some of Oxford's famous museums and libraries.

6. Follow links to locate web pages about the **Ashmolean Museum**, the **Pitt Rivers Museum** and the **Bodleian Library**.

7. Bookmark each of the pages and print copies of them.

While in Oxford, you want to visit one of the famous Colleges.

8. From the University's home page, follow a link to take you to a page listing all the colleges.

9. Choose a college and click on its link. This will take you to that college's web page. Browse this page to find any information that interests you.

Searching the Internet

There's so much information on the Internet... but you won't always know where it is.
That's why you need search engines — they find things for you.

There are Loads of Different Search Engines

A search engine is a type of website that is used to find other websites for you.
You get to it by typing in an address, just like any website.
Here are the addresses of a few search engines:

www.google.com	www.google.co.uk
www.yahoo.com	uk.yahoo.com
www.altavista.com	uk.altavista.com
www.excite.com	www.excite.co.uk

These are the UK versions of these search engines.

All You Do is Type in a Word

This is what the 'Google' search engine looks like. (Most search engines look fairly similar.)
All you do is:

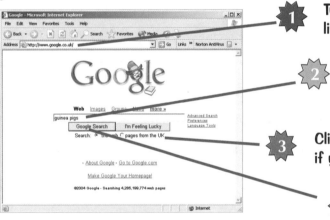

1 Type in the address of a good search engine, like Google, then press Enter.

2 Click in the search box. Now, type in whatever you want to search for information about. Say, guinea pigs.

3 Click on the circle next to 'pages from the UK' if you only want to find UK-based websites.

4 Click on 'Search'. (On other search engines it might be 'Go'.)

The search engine looks through a massive database of websites.
It comes up with a list of pages which mention what you're searching for.
(It'll also show a bit of the page itself.)

5 Look at the list and decide which result is most likely to contain the information you need.
Then click on its underlined title (the hyperlink) to go to that webpage.

Google can't find you handsome millionaires...

It's quite likely that the first website you try won't give you the information you want.
Well, never mind. Just click on 'Back' (at the top left of the screen) and try a different one.

Searching the Internet

You might not always find what you want straight away. Here's how to refine your search.

You Can Make Your Search Specific

Imagine you wanted to find out whether guinea pigs will eat sweetcorn...

You could type in 'guinea pigs' — you'd find out lots of things about guinea pigs, but you wouldn't necessarily find the answer to your question.

So what you should do is...

1 Search for the words that you want to see together on a web page — in this case, 'guinea pig' and 'sweetcorn'.

2 Look at your results — there are quite a few that look like they answer the question. Click on one to go to it.

Some Search Engines Offer an 'Advanced Search'

It's possible to refine your search even more, if you want to.
Most search engines offer an advanced search, which lets you look for really specific things.

Imagine, for example, you wanted to find out which spiders have a deadly bite, but when you searched under 'spider', you kept finding Spider-Man websites. You should...

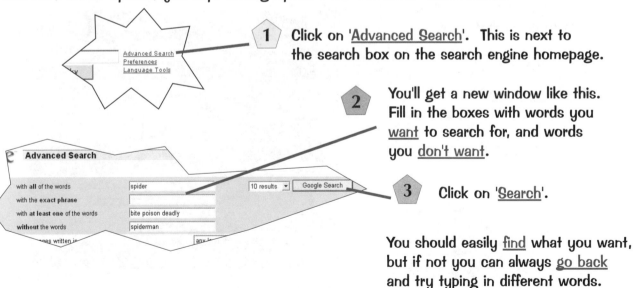

1 Click on 'Advanced Search'. This is next to the search box on the search engine homepage.

2 You'll get a new window like this. Fill in the boxes with words you want to search for, and words you don't want.

3 Click on 'Search'.

You should easily find what you want, but if not you can always go back and try typing in different words.

I'm still searching for true love...

When you're doing your assessment, you'll be asked to find some information. Don't just find a search engine's list of sites — actually go to one of the sites and print out the information.

Searching Websites

It's not only search engines that help you find information on the Internet.

Some Websites Have Their Own Search Facility

Some websites are so <u>big</u> and <u>complex</u> that it's hard to find the information you want in them. That's why some have their own <u>search facility</u> to help you look for things in the website.

The Natural History Museum website is a good example — below is its homepage.

1 Go to the Natural History Museum's website at: **www.nhm.ac.uk**

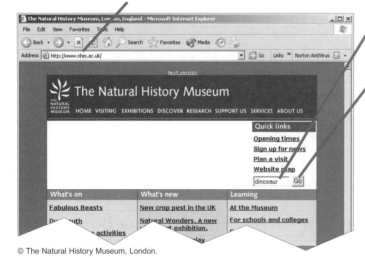

© The Natural History Museum, London.

2 Click your mouse in the box. Then <u>type</u> in what you'd like to look for — try 'dinosaur'.

3 Click on '<u>Go</u>' (or '<u>Search</u>').

You'll get a page of <u>results</u>, like you did from a search engine.

The results will be listed in <u>order</u> of how good a match they are. Best match first.

(These results even have a <u>star rating</u> to show how good a match they are.)

4 As with a search engine, just <u>click</u> on the underlined title to go to that page.

5 If you <u>don't like</u> the page you've been sent to, and want to go back to the <u>list</u> of results, just click on '<u>Back</u>'.

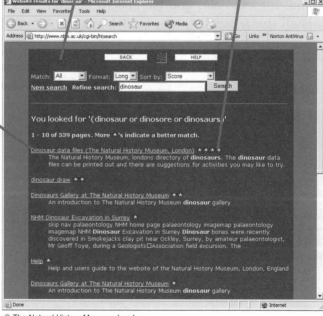

© The Natural History Museum, London.

Click, type, click, click — not hard...

So now you know how to find things through a search engine and the search bit of a website. Just think of all that stuff waiting to be found out — and you now know how to find it.

Selecting Appropriate Material

It's easy to find wads of information on the Internet, but be careful about trusting it entirely...

Don't Trust Everything You Read on the Internet

Anyone can make a website, and any information can get on the Internet:

People are likely to create a website if they've got a point to make
— about a controversial issue like fox-hunting, for example.
They'll put information on their website to support their point,
but that makes it biased. You don't get both sides of the story.

You'll also find information on the Internet that's just wrong. People write lies and make mistakes about things all the time.

The Internet also holds lots of material that people might find offensive, e.g. pornography, and material that is illegal. There are Internet monitors out there trying to find and close down illegal sites, but there are so many sites that it's impossible to keep them under control.

So, before you believe what you read:

1) Think about who created the website and why. How trustworthy are they?

2) Try to get your information from a reputable website.
Educational organisations and museums tend to have websites that try to be fair.

3) Use other websites to double-check the information you find.

Things on the Internet Have Copyright

Remember, stuff on the Internet often has copyright and you might have to pay to quote it.

If you want to copy chunks of text from the Internet for an academic reason, like a college essay, then that's fine.
You just have to quote your source — say where it came from.

But — if you want to copy things off the Internet for a business reason, you'll have to ask permission from the website's owner. They might say fine, or no, or they might charge you some money. But you have to ask permission or you could get sued.

Elvis is ALIVE — I've seen his website...

It's important to realise that although the Internet is known as the "information superhighway", not all the "information" you find is necessarily true. It's up to you to decide if you trust it.

Saving Web Pages

You can save a copy of a whole web page or just one part of it, onto your computer.
Then you can view it whenever you like without connecting to the Internet.

You can Save Web Pages on your Computer

 Open 'Internet Explorer'.

 Go to a website. I've used www.number-10.gov.uk/output/page43.asp , but you can use any website you like.

 When the web page has loaded, click on the 'File' menu, move your mouse down, then click on 'Save as'.

© Crown Copyright

Stan had forgotten to save the web page he needed for his project.

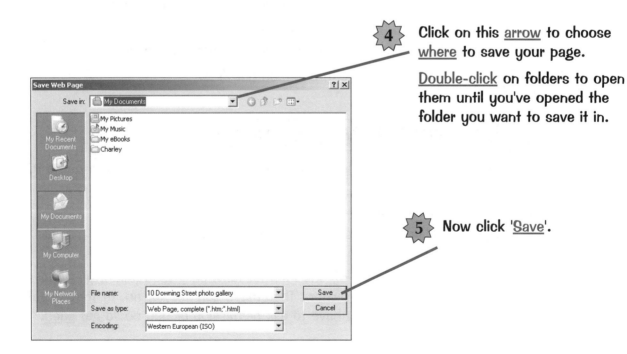

4 Click on this arrow to choose where to save your page.

Double-click on folders to open them until you've opened the folder you want to save it in.

5 Now click 'Save'.

Websites can disappear...

If you save a web page on your computer it won't matter if the website changes, or is removed altogether. Remember that you are only saving the current page, not the whole website.

Saving Pictures

If there's a picture or photo on a website that you really like and want to keep, you can <u>save it</u>.

Saving a <u>Picture</u> is a bit <u>Different</u>

 1 On the website, find the picture or photo that you want to save.
Click on it with your <u>right</u> mouse button (yep, <u>right</u> mouse button again).

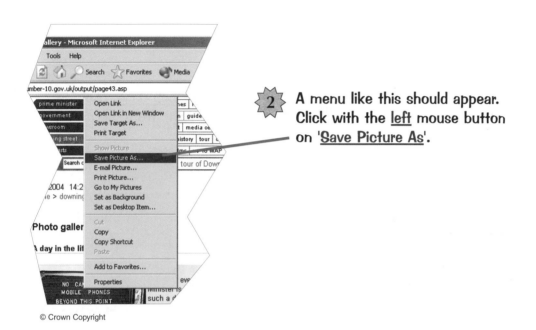

© Crown Copyright

2 A menu like this should appear.
Click with the <u>left</u> mouse button
on '<u>Save Picture As</u>'.

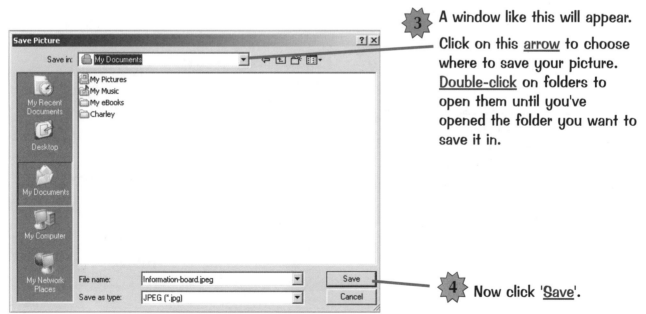

3 A window like this will appear.

Click on this <u>arrow</u> to choose
where to save your picture.
<u>Double-click</u> on folders to
open them until you've
opened the folder you want to
save it in.

4 Now click '<u>Save</u>'.

You'll be amazed at what you can find...

You'll have no problem finding all sorts of useful (or fun) things to save from the Internet.
Whatever you're interested in, you'll find something to keep you entertained.

Printing Web Pages

If you like paper copies of things, you can print a web page.

You can Print Whole Web Pages...

 Open 'Internet Explorer'.

 Go to a website. I've used www.nhm.ac.uk .
Wait for the page to load.

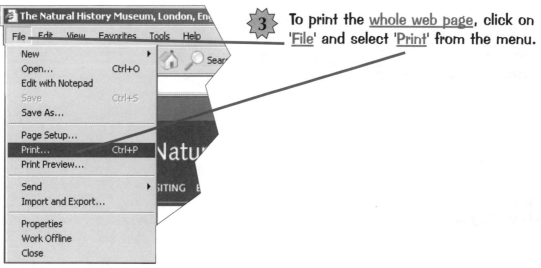

To print the whole web page, click on 'File' and select 'Print' from the menu.

© The Natural History Museum, London.

 A print menu like this will appear. Check that the correct printer is selected and that it's set to print the right number of copies.

When you're happy with the options, click on 'Print'.

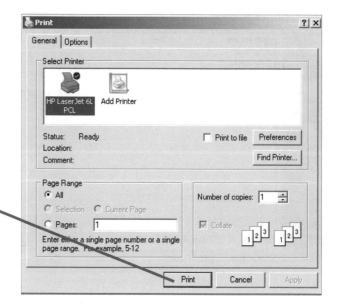

Still waiting for some handsome prints...

You might notice that some web pages you print out look different to what's on the screen. Well, don't panic. It's the same thing — it's just arranged a bit differently to print out OK.

Printing Web Pages

...Or Just Print Part of a Web Page

 Click on one of the photos with your right mouse button.

 Move your mouse over the menu and click on 'Print Picture'.

Geoff believes one-to-one training gets the best out of his staff.

© Crown Copyright

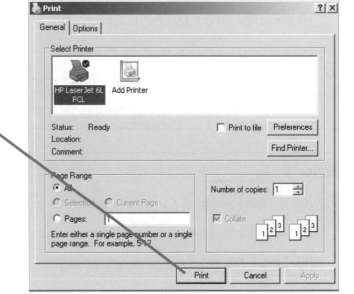

7 When you see this window, check the options look right, then click on 'Print'.

8 When it's finished printing, close 'Internet Explorer'.

Printing is just the most fascinating thing...

Actually it's not, I was lying. Do this exercise again and find a much more exciting picture to print out instead. Something with a camel, some trifle and Big Ben should do it.

Section Five — Practice Exercises

There are three little practice exercises to do on this page — give them a try.

Exercise 1

1.   Access the NHS Direct website at www.nhsdirect.nhs.uk

2.   Using the search facility on this website, find a web page with information about **hay fever**.

3.   Bookmark this page and print out the information.

4.   Go back to the home page on the NHS Direct website.

5.   Using the search facility on the website, find information about **prevention of back pain**.

6.   Save this page of information and print one copy.

Exercise 2

1.   Access the Met Office website at www.meto.gov.uk

2.   Using the search facility on the website, find a page about the **long hot summer** of **1976**. Bookmark the page and print out the information

3.   A friend of yours says that 2003 felt even hotter than 1976.
      Use the search facility to locate pages giving a **monthly weather summary** for **2003**.
      Find a page which gives temperature summaries.
      Read through this information to find out if your friend is correct.
      Bookmark the page and print out the information.

4.   Now use the search facility on this website to find **webcam** images.

5.   Save the page with the webcam images.

6.   Find a 5-day **regional forecast** for your region.

   A webcam is a small camera that is connected to a website to show live, moving images.

7.   Bookmark this page and print out this information.

Exercise 3

1.   Access the Foreign & Commonwealth Office website at www.fco.gov.uk

2.   Use the search facility on the website to find travel advice for **Tanzania**.

3.   Bookmark this page and print out the information.

4.   Now use the search facility to find information about another country that interests you.

5.   Save this page of information.

Section Five — Practice Exercises

Now it's time for a couple of really searching exercises...

Exercise 4

Your tutor would like information about the different strategies that students use to learn.

1.   Use a web-based search engine to search for a web page about **learning styles**
      (**visual**, **auditory**, **kinesthetic**).

2.   Follow the links to find a web page on this topic.

3.   Bookmark this page.

4.   Print the web page containing the information.

Your tutor would also like information about team work, especially the ideas by Dr Meredith Belbin.

5.   Use a web-based search engine to search for a web page
      about **team work** and **Dr Meredith Belbin**.

6.   Follow the links to find a web page on this topic.

7.   Bookmark this page.

8.   Print the web page containing the information.

Exercise 5

You want to plan a weekend trip to Paris, France.

1.   Use a web-based search engine to search for a web page about **Paris** and its historical sites.
      Find information about the **Louvre** (art gallery), the **Eiffel Tower** and the **Arc de Triomphe**.
      (The pages must be in English.)

2.   For each of the three sites above, print a web page containing information about it.

3.   Find a map of Paris which has the three sites on it.

You may want to go to Disneyland Paris (Euro Disney) for a day trip.

4.   Use a web-based search engine to find websites about **Disneyland Paris**.

5.   Locate pages that contain information on the opening times, admission prices,
      and how to get there. Print out the web pages containing this information.

Advice for the Assessment

Once you've <u>completed</u> the course, you're ready to take the <u>assessment</u>.
Here's a bit of <u>advice</u> to help you prepare for it.
You've probably seen it before, but read it again — it's <u>useful stuff</u>.

You'll get 2 Hours to Complete the Assessment

You've got <u>plenty</u> of time to do the assessment, so...

- Don't <u>panic</u>.

  - Don't <u>rush</u> — you'll make mistakes.

    - Read the <u>instructions</u> properly, and make sure you <u>follow</u> them.

      - <u>Check</u> your work as you go along, especially your <u>typing</u>.

        - <u>Don't</u> panic.

Avoid these Errors

If you make a really <u>big error</u>, like not doing one of the <u>tasks</u> in the assessment, you <u>won't pass</u>.
So, make sure you follow the instructions <u>carefully</u>.

If you make <u>more than three</u> minor errors, you won't pass the assessment either.
So, <u>avoid</u> making small mistakes like these:

1) Making a <u>typing</u> (<u>data entry</u>) error in the data you're asked to enter.
   You get <u>one error</u> for each incorrect word in the assessment.

2) Creating a <u>new</u> e-mail message when you're asked to forward or reply to one.

3) Saving the <u>whole</u> web page when you've been asked to save a <u>picture</u>.

Watch Out for Accuracy Errors

When you're entering e-mail and Internet addresses, <u>make sure</u> you type them
<u>exactly</u> as they're written, or they won't work, and you'll be throwing marks away.

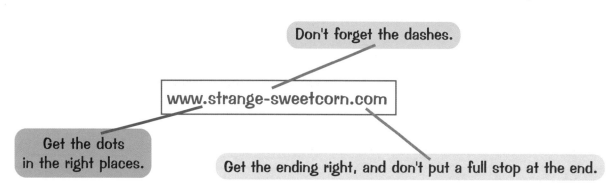

Don't forget the dashes.

www.strange-sweetcorn.com

Get the dots
in the right places.

Get the ending right, and don't put a full stop at the end.

Just take a few deep breaths and you'll be fine...

If you've prepared for the assessment properly, you'll be just fine.
All the skills you need are in this book, so just get out there and show what you can do.

Advice for the Assessment

Check that you Know How to Do these Things

All you need to know to pass the assessment is in this book.
Use the checklist below to make sure you're confident with all the tasks you could
be asked to do. Go back and look at the relevant pages again if you're not sure.

1)	Create e-mail messages.		Page 11
2)	Receive and read e-mail messages.		Page 12
3)	Reply to e-mails.		Page 13
4)	Forward e-mails.		Page 14
5)	Store and retrieve an e-mail address.		Page 15-18
6)	Delete e-mails.		Pages 21
7)	Print e-mails.		Page 22
8)	Send an e-mail with an attachment.		Pages 23
9)	Receive and store an e-mail attachment.		Page 24-25
10)	Access a specified web page using its address.		Page 29
11)	Navigate the World Wide Web using hyperlinks.		Page 30
12)	Store a web address.		Page 32
13)	Use a general web search engine.		Page 36-37
14)	Use a site-specific web search engine.		Pages 38
15)	Save data from a web page.		Pages 40-41
16)	Print a web page or part of a web page.		Pages 42-43

You're nearly there, keep going... not far now...

If you've ticked all the boxes, you should be ready for a practice assessment.
Try the one over the page and see how you get on.

Practice Assessment

To start this assessment, you need to send an e-mail with "assessment" as the subject heading to a fictional editor whose e-mail address is "clait@cgpbooks.co.uk". You can leave the message blank, but you <u>must get the subject right</u>. You will receive an e-mail and attachment from the 'editor' to be used in the assessment.

Tutors: If you wish to send the attachment to your students yourself, the text for the e-mail and the image file are included on the CD.

Scenario

You are starting a new job, working as an Administrative Assistant for CGP Books.

You are helping your editor to create a new book series.

Your editor has sent you an e-mail about a new book cover.

1. Open your mailbox and read the message from clait@cgpbooks.co.uk

    Add this e-mail address to your address book.

    Print a copy of the attached file, **tiger.gif**

You need to inform the graphics team of these details.

2. Prepare to forward the message and its attachment to wildlifegraphics@cgpbooks.co.uk, adding the following text:

    Here is the provisional cover photograph for the tiger book.
    Please can you take a look at it and let me know what you think of it?

    Add your name and centre number to the end of your message.

    Check your message for errors and, making sure your e-mail system saves outgoing messages, forward the e-mail message including the attachment.

You should let your editor know that you have received the message.

3. Prepare a reply to the editor with the following message:

    Thank you for sending the photograph.
    I have contacted the Graphics team and will let you know their opinion as soon as possible.

    Add your name and centre number to the end of your message.

    Check your message for errors and, making sure your e-mail system saves outgoing messages, send the reply.

You need to manage your mailbox to reduce storage demands.

4. Save the attachment **tiger.gif** separately from the mailbox and delete the original message from your incoming mail folder only.

Practice Assessment

The editor needs some information on the number of Siberian tigers left in the wild.

5. Use a web-based search engine to search for a web page about **Siberian tigers**. Follow links to find a web page with information about the number of these tigers in the wild.

    Bookmark the page.

    Print the web page containing the information.

Your editor also wants information on other books about tigers.

6. Access the following website: www.amazon.co.uk

    Follow the links to the search page. Use the local search facility to locate a page on the site showing the front cover of a book about **tigers**.

    Bookmark the web page.

    Print a copy of the web page containing the information.

    Save the picture of the front cover as **competitor.jpg**

7. Prepare an e-mail message to your editor using the address stored in your address book. Give the message the subject **Competitors' Tiger Books**.

    Type the following message:

    Here is a picture of the front cover of one of our competitor's books on tigers. Let me know if you need any more help.

    Add your name and centre number to the end of your message.

    Locate and attach a copy of the file **competitor.jpg** saved at step 6.

    Make sure a copy of your e-mail message will be sent to the graphics department at wildlifegraphics@cgpbooks.co.uk

    Check your message for errors and, making sure your system saves outgoing messages, send the e-mail message and attachment.

8. Locate the copies of the three e-mail messages you have sent and print a copy of each message. Make sure header details (To, From, Date, Subject) are shown on all e-mail printouts. Make sure attachment details are shown where appropriate (steps 2 and 7).

9. Access the bookmark facility and ask your tutor to check the stored URLs.

10. Exit the software securely.

Index